BERKLEE PRESS

SAXOPHONE

SOUND EFFECTS

To access audio visit:
www.halleonard.com/mylibrary

Enter Code
1407-9704-7425-4261

**CIRCULAR BREATHING,
MULTIPHONICS,
ALTISSIMO
REGISTER PLAYING,
AND MUCH MORE!**

Edited by Jonathan Feist

UELI DÖRIG

For my beautiful Claudia

Berklee Press

Vice President: David Kusek
Dean of Continuing Education: Debbie Cavalier
Assistant Vice President of Operations/CFO: Robert F. Green
Managing Editor: Jonathan Feist
Editorial Assistants: David Hume, Won (Sara) Hwang
Cover Designer: Kathy Kikkert
Cover Photo: Martin Cavé

All compositions by Ueli Dörig. Recorded and mixed by Matt MacKinnon in Ottawa, Canada.
Alto saxophone played by Ueli Dörig. Playback production by Dörig Music.
Visit www.uelidoerig.com for more information.

ISBN 978-0-87639-127-3

1140 Boylston Street
Boston, MA 02215-3693 USA
(617) 747-2146

Visit Berklee Press Online at
www.berkleepress.com

DISTRIBUTED BY

HAL•LEONARD®

7777 W. BLUEMOUND RD. P.O. BOX 13819
MILWAUKEE, WISCONSIN 53213

Visit Hal Leonard Online at
www.halleonard.com

CONTENTS

AUDIO TRACKS

Part I. Technique

Track	Title	Technique
01	Inhaling and Exhaling Noise	01
02	Finger Clicking Noise	02
03	Finger Clicking and Playing	02
04	Key Clapping	03
05	Key Damping	03
06	Laughing Saxophone	04
07	False Fingerings	05
08	Low "A"	06
09	Damping Low B♭ to A	06
10	Regular Vibrato	07
11	Irregular Vibrato	07
12	The Adderley Trill	08
13	Mouthpiece Only	09
14	"Flax"	09
15	"Flunet"	09
16	Wah-wah and Distortion	10
17	Ghost Notes	11
18	Growling	12
19	Singing Sound of the Growl	12
20	Quarter Tones	13
21	Double Tonguing	14
22	Triple Tonguing	14
23	Flutter Tonguing	15
24	Rolling "R"	15
25	Harmonics and Overtones	16
26	Multiphonics	17
27	Altissimo Register	18
28	Circular Breathing	19

Part II. Etudes

Track	Title
29	"The Elephant" Performance
30	"The Elephant" E♭ Play Along
31	"The Elephant" B♭ Play Along
32	"The Bacteria" Performance
33	"The Bacteria" E♭ Play Along
34	"The Bacteria" B♭ Play Along
35	"The Hornets" Performance
36	"The Hornets" E♭ Play Along
37	"The Hornets" B♭ Play Along
38	"The Whale" Performance
39	"The Whale" E♭ Play Along
40	"The Whale" B♭ Play Along
41	"The Horse" Performance
42	"The Horse" E♭ Play Along
43	"The Horse" B♭ Play Along
44	"The Mosquito" Performance
45	"The Mosquito" E♭ Play Along
46	"The Mosquito" B♭ Play Along
47	"The Shark" Performance
48	"The Shark" E♭ Play Along
49	"The Shark" B♭ Play Along
50	"The Vampire Bat" Performance
51	"The Vampire Bat" E♭ Play Along
52	"The Vampire Bat" B♭ Play Along
53	"The Cobra" Performance
54	"The Cobra" E♭ Play Along
55	"The Cobra" B♭ Play Along

Recorded and mixed by Matt MacKinnon in Ottawa, Canada.

INTRODUCTION

This book will make you a stronger player by putting you out of your comfort zone and by exposing you to new and challenging situations. These sound effects will help you to build flexibility, strength, and endurance.

Experience through Experimentation

Experimentation leads to experience. Working on these sound effects will help you to enhance the knowledge of your body and your instrument. With every effect you learn you gain more control over your body and instrument. The more control we have, the more freedom we have to do whatever we want to do.

Six Key Elements

To make a sound effect work you have to consider the following six key elements:

1. Embouchure
2. Airstream
3. Mouthpiece Intake
4. Opening of the Throat
5. Dynamics
6. Tongue position

Listening

Concentrate on listening to what you are doing. Your ears will guide you through the process of experimentation. They will tell you if you are going in the right direction. Be patient. It is normal that learning these techniques takes some time. Sometimes, it even takes a lot of time. Recording yourself and listening to the recording is a great way to enhance the quality of your practice time.

How to Use This Book

There are two main sections in this book. The first one is about *learning* sound effects and the second one is about *applying* them. The special effects in the first section are organized going from easy to difficult.

How to Use Sound Effects

Using sound effects is like using spices while cooking. If you apply the right amount of spices, you might be considered a good chef. But always remember: Too much spice can ruin even the simplest dish! It is one thing to be capable of playing a special effect and another to use it in a tasteful way. This book will help you with the first part and the recommended listening in this book with the second part.

Octave Notation

Reading the Fingering Charts

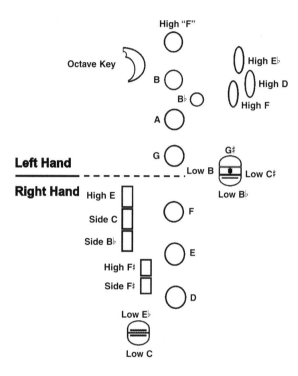

PART I

Technique

1. INHALING AND EXHALING NOISE

TRACK 1

Breathing through your saxophone can sound like ocean waves or wind blowing through trees. These breath effects don't require you to finger notes on your saxophone. Rather than inhaling through your nose, breathe in and out through your mouthpiece. Cover almost the whole reed with your tongue, and take deep breaths through the mouthpiece. Exhale in the same position. Experiment doing this with different fingerings.

Amplify Quiet Effects

Some effects, such as these breathing effects, are by nature very quiet. Therefore, amplify the sound, using a directional microphone pointed just below the last held-down key.

2. FINGER CLICKING

TRACK 2   TRACK 3

You can produce the sound of raindrops hitting a window and similar impressions by clicking with your fingernails on the bell of your saxophone. Another possibility is to play your saxophone using only your left hand and clicking a rhythm with your right-hand fingernails.

Mic Technique

To mic this effect, point a directional microphone at the bell of your saxophone because of the low volume of this effect.

3. KEY CLAPPING AND DAMPING

Clapping

TRACK 4

Clapping effects are made using just key sounds, rather than blowing through your horn. Just move your fingers rhythmically.

Clapping 1.   Press the fingering for low C and then add very quickly and strongly the low B♭ key with your left hand pinky.

Clapping 2.   Press the fingering for low G. Add very quickly and strongly the three fingers to get to the low D fingering.

Clapping 3.   Start with no keys pressed. Add very quickly and strongly the right hand pinky, and press the low C key.

There are endless combinations you can discover through experimentation.

Clapping Mic Technique
Point a directional microphone towards the involved keys.

Damping

TRACK 5

The damping effect changes your sound in two ways. At first, after closing your key about halfway, you will hear your note muted to a certain degree. If you continue to close your key a bit more, you will realize that the note starts to bend down.

Step 1.   Play an A² and move gently up and down your G key but never close it completely. Listen to how the volume diminishes. Then, observe how your A² starts to bend down towards G².

Step 2.   Produce a regular vibrato using this effect with A² (check out the section on vibrato to see what "regular vibrato" is).

Step 3.   Try the same thing on different notes in different octaves.

Practice with a Metronome
Use a metronome when you practice regular vibrato. Keep your beats even.

4. LAUGHING SAXOPHONE

TRACK 6

The laughing saxophone effect consists of three parts. First, start the note with the articulation "ku," and play the note on pitch. Then change the articulation to "ah" during the second part of the note, and bend it down. Third, play a series of descending notes with the articulation "kuah, kuah, kuah, kuah!"

Laughing Research
You want this effect to sound as close to a human laugh as possible. Therefore listen carefully to how people laugh.

5. FALSE FINGERINGS

TRACK 7

False fingerings produce a different sound quality or timbre than the regular fingering for the same note. This becomes more obvious when a false fingering is being played right after the regular fingering for the same note. Don't worry, if the false fingering sound is slightly out of tune, as this is part of the effect.

Be aware that false fingerings *are not* the same as "alternative" fingerings. Alternative fingerings share the same sound quality or timbre with the regular fingering of the same note. Their purpose is to offer a smoother fingering for certain fast note combinations.

Regular Fingering	False Fingering
B^2	Play B^1 with the octave key.
C^2	Play C^1 with the octave key.
$C\#^2/D\flat^3$	Play $C\#^1/D\flat^2$ with the octave key.
D^3	Play D^2 without the octave key.
$D\#^3/E\flat^3$	Play high E^4 without the octave key.
E^3	Play E^3 and add the low C key with the pinky of the right hand.
F^3	Play 2nd harmonic of $B\flat^1$. Check out technique 16, "Harmonics and Overtones."
$F\#^3$	Play 2nd harmonic of B^1.
G^3	Play 2nd harmonic of C^1.
$G\#^3/A\flat^3$	Play 2nd harmonic of $C\#^1$.
A^3	Play A^3 and add the three fingers of the right hand.
$A\#^3/B\flat^3$	Play $A\#^3/B\flat^3$ and add the three fingers of the right hand.
B^3	Play B^3 and add the lowest of the three side keys of the right hand.
C^3	Play C^3 and add the three fingers of the right hand.
$C\#^3/D\flat^4$	Play $C\#^3/D\flat^4$ and add the three fingers of the right hand.

Artists Who Use False Fingering Effects

Eric Marienthal
Joshua Redman
Michael Brecker

6. LOW A

TRACK 8   TRACK 9

Play your low B♭. Turn the bell of your saxophone towards the upper part of your left leg. Use your leg as a damper and cover a part of your saxophone's bell. This should lower your B♭ to a low A.

Fig. 6.1. Low A

7. VIBRATO

There are several different types of vibrato and ways to create vibrato effects.

Variation of Rate

Variation of rate refers to the speed of the vibration. In notation, this can either be described with words such as "fast vibrato" or with rhythmic value such as "sixteenth note vibrato."

Variation of Width

Variation of width refers to the degree of the vibrato. The range can be from a hint of a vibrato to a very dramatic and big vibrato.

Diaphragm Technique (Volume Vibrato)

Vibrato can result from changing the air support controlled by the diaphragm. The peak of the vibrato happens when the air pressure is at its highest. The bottom of the vibrato happens when the air pressure is at its lowest.

Embouchure Technique (Pitch Vibrato)

Vibrato can also be created by changing tightness of the embouchure. The peak of the vibrato happens when the embouchure is the tightest and therefore the pitch is the highest. The bottom of the vibrato happens when the embouchure is the loosest and therefore the pitch is the lowest.

Closing Keys Halfway Technique or Key Damping (Pitch Vibrato)

Changing the saxophone keys can also result in vibrato. Play a G^2. Experiment with closing the F♯ key (middle finger of the right hand) to different degrees. When the key is almost closed, it bends the G^2 slightly down. By moving your finger slightly back and forth in that narrow margin, you can create a vibrato. The faster you move your finger, the higher the rate of the vibrato. Try it on other notes, too.

Regular Vibrato

TRACK 10

Regular (or "even") vibrato has the same rate over time. It doesn't speed up nor slow down. Regular vibrato is characteristic of classical music. Listen to opera singers such as Maria Callas to learn how this effect is done in a musical and tasteful way.

Irregular Vibrato

TRACK 11

Contrary to the regular vibrato, *irregular* vibrato speeds up or slows down. Listen to jazz singers such as Ella Fitzgerald for effective examples of irregular vibrato.

Vibrato Tips
- Use a metronome when practicing regular vibrato.
- As a soloist, you can use whatever vibrato you want, but when playing in a horn section, it is important that all the players of the section use the same vibrato.

Artists Who Use a Lot of Vibrato
Sidney Bechet
Dexter Gordon
Maria Callas
Ella Fitzgerald

8. TRILLS

Experiment trilling notes using different (side) keys. The most popular one is the highest of the three side keys on the right side, but there are many more to discover.

The Adderley Trill

One very popular combination of trills is called the *Adderley trill* (named after Cannonball Adderley). To perform this trill:

- Move chromatically up starting on G^3 and end on $D\#^4/E\flat^4$.

- Trill fast with the highest of the three side keys (high E^4 key) in your right hand while going upward.

- Bend each note first down, then up. If done properly, the notes will seem to blend together.

Embouchure Tip
Start the first note of the trill with a loose embouchure. This way, you can bend it up easier.

Artists Who Use Trills
Cannonball Adderley
King Curtis

9. MOUTHPIECE, NECK, AND HYBRID INSTRUMENTS

Mouthpiece

Put the reed on your mouthpiece, and blow. You can get different sounds by entering your pinky through the open side of the mouthpiece to varying degrees.

Neck

Same as "Mouthpiece," described above, but adding the neck to your mouthpiece.

Hybrid Instruments

A *hybrid instrument* is an instrument made up from parts of at least two different instruments.

"Flax"

TRACK 14

Replace the flute's headjoint with a soprano sax mouthpiece and its neck. Wrap some painter's tape around the spot where they connect, and you are ready to go.

"Flunet"

TRACK 15

While not technically a "saxophone effect," this is another good hybrid instrument to try if you double on flute and clarinet. Replace the flute's headjoint with the two top parts of a clarinet. The clarinet parts will be a little bit too large to fit perfectly on the flute. You can fill in the gap with some paper. Fold a small piece of paper, wrap it around the top of the flute, and put the clarinet mouthpiece back on.

More Hybrids

All you need for further experimentation is a sound production device (mouthpiece) and a controller (instrument body with holes for fingerings).

10. ELECTRONIC EFFECTS

TRACK 16

Using a microphone when playing the saxophone opens a whole world of electronic possibilities. The signal can then be modified by an external filter or computer sound effects generator. These are more commonly designed for other instruments, particularly guitar, but you can also use them on a microphone. Such effects include distortion, delay, tremolo, wah-wah, fuzz, reverb, and many more. It's a lot of fun experimenting with these effects while playing, but it's also possible to apply them after you played in a recording studio or with some music software.

Guitarist Advice on Effects

Electronic effects are widely used by electric guitar players. Talk to them about how to use these effects in a tasteful way.

11. GHOST NOTES

Contrary to accented notes, ghost notes are de-emphasized and almost silent. Functioning as a rhythmic placeholder, ghost notes can be described as something between an unaccented note and a rest, leaning more towards the rest. A ghost note is played for the full length of its rhythmic value and not to be mixed up with grace notes.

Tongue the note you want to make a ghost note, and keep the tip of your tongue on one half of the reed. This way, you are using your tongue as a damper. Experiment to find where exactly to put your tongue to make the sound of a ghost note. If you can't hear any sound, you are probably covering too much of the reed. If your note is too loud, however, then you are probably not covering enough of the reed.

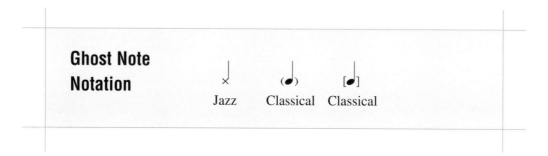

Ghost Note Notation

Jazz   Classical   Classical

Ghost Note Practice
Alternate between ghosted and normal notes when practicing ghost notes.

Artists Who Play Ghost Notes

Charlie Parker
David Sanborn

12. GROWLING

To make a growl sound, you can sing, hum, or scream into the mouthpiece while playing a note. You can also put some saliva on the top back of your tongue and roll it. As you are experimenting, you will discover that it is more difficult to growl in the lower octave of the saxophone. Try to vary the degree of aggressiveness of your growl.

Mic Technique for Growls
If you growl during a recording session, be sure the microphone doesn't pick up the vocal sound.

Artists Who Use Growl Sounds

Ben Webster
Illinois Jacquet
Earl Bostic

13. QUARTER TONES

TRACK 20

A quarter tone is a note that's located between two semitones. Therefore, there is a possible quarter tone between every step in the chromatic scale. They can be achieved by bending a note from the chromatic scale or by using special fingerings.

And so on...

Chromatic Scale	C		C#/D♭		D		D#/E♭		E		F	
Quarter Tones		C1/4# D3/4♭		D1/4♭ C3/4#		D1/4# E3/4♭		E1/4♭ D3/4#		E1/4# F1/4♭		F1/4# G3/4♭

Good Opportunities for Using Quarter Tones

Experiment using quarter tones in harmonic minor, blues, and pentatonic scales as well as chromatic passages.

¼ sharp ‡ or ♯ or ⧺   ¼ flat ꝭ or ♭ or ♮

sharp ♯   flat ♭

¾ sharp ♯ or ‡   ¾ flat ꝭ or ♭ or ♭♭

Artists Who Use Quarter Tones

Middle eastern music
Mikhail Mishaqa
Charles Ives

The quarter tone fingerings in this book are the fingerings that I found to be the easiest to play. Remember: *My* best fingerings might not be *your* best fingerings. That's why you can find blank fingering charts for copying purposes in Appendix A. I strongly recommend using them for experimentation.

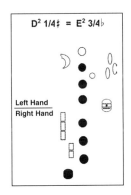

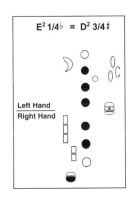

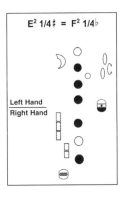

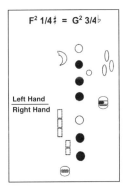

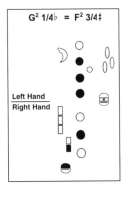

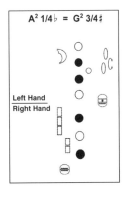

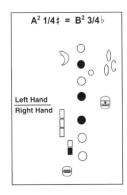

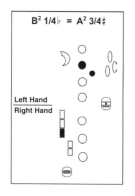 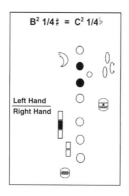 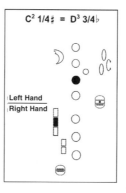 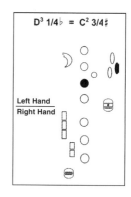

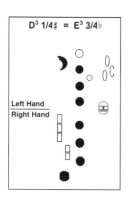 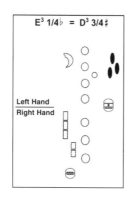 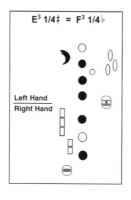 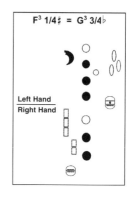

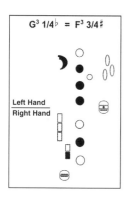  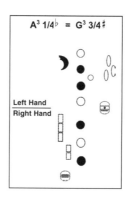 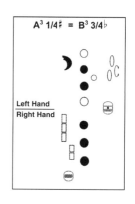

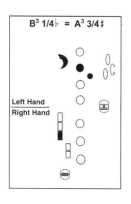 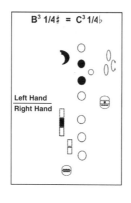 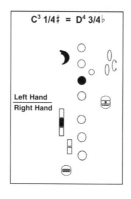 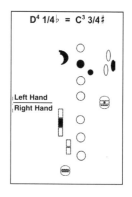

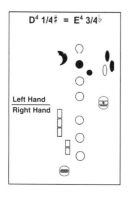 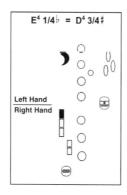 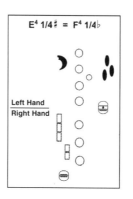

Use the blank fingering charts on page 25 to expand above F4 1/4♭ through experimentation.

14. DOUBLE AND TRIPLE TONGUING

TRACK 21 TRACK 22

Double and triple tonguings allow us to stop the airflow faster than single tonguing. This can be quite useful when we need to play a fast pizzicato or staccato passage (like in classical music). Additionally, double and triple tonguings are physically less demanding than fast single tonguing and therefore cause less fatigue. Use double tonguing when passages are too fast for single tonguing and triple tonguing when passages are too fast for double tonguing.

	Hard Articulation	Soft Articulation
Single Tonguing	Ta	Da
Double Tonguing	Ta Ka	Da Ga
Triple Tonguing	Ta Ka Ta	Da Ga Da

Use these steps to practice double and triple tonguing.

Step 1. Practice the articulation without your saxophone. Try to realize how the "Ta" and "Da" are happening *on the reed*, whereas the "Ka" and "Ga" are happening *on the roof of your mouth.*

Step 2. Try to play the notes in the middle register of your saxophone using the articulation Ta, Da, Ka, and Ga. Play one note at a time. Pay attention to how they sound and how they feel.

Step 3. Put the following articulation together: Ta Ka and Da Ga. Play them together at a very slow tempo. If your ears tell you that you are playing them correctly, speed them up, bit by bit, until you reach a fast tempo.

Step 4. Repeat step 3 with the articulations Ta Ka Ta and Da Ga Da.

Step 5. Double and triple tongue in all registers at different speeds using a metronome.

Step 6. Double and triple tongue while playing scales and melodies.

More Syllables for Tonguing

Experiment with different syllables. Replace: Ta with Tu, Too, Tah; Ka with Ku, Koo, Kuh; Da with Du, Doo, Duh; Ga with Gu, Goo, and Guh. Listen to how the sound changes.

Artists Who Use Double and Triple Tonguings

James Moody
Johnny Griffin

15. FLUTTER TONGUING

TRACK 23 TRACK 24

To produce the flutter-tongue effect, you must produce a rolling "R." Start practicing the flutter tongue without the saxophone. Try to sound like a ringing telephone or a cat's purr. To flutter tongue with the saxophone, you have to play and roll Rs at the same time. You can also flutter tongue with different articulations. Experiment with: **tr**rrrrr, **dr**rrrrr, **fr**rrrrr, and more. You might find it helpful to take less of the mouthpiece in your mouth while doing this.

Avoid the Reed
Pay attention not to touch the reed with your tongue while flutter tonguing!

Artists Who Use Flutter Tonguing

King Curtis
Lee Allen

16. HARMONICS AND OVERTONES

TRACK 25

Beyond their use as sound effects, working on harmonics and overtones is a great way to increase your sound quality. It is also a great preliminary exercise for altissimo and false-fingering playing. Play a note in the low register of your saxophone (e.g., $B\flat^1$, B^1, C^1). Experiment with increasing the air support and redirecting the airstream, but don't tighten your embouchure to get higher and higher notes. These notes are called "harmonics" or "overtones." The lowest note that corresponds to the fingering is called the "fundamental" or "first (1st) harmonic."

1st Harmonic	=	Fundamental
2nd Harmonic	=	1st Overtone
3rd Harmonic	=	2nd Overtone
4th Harmonic	=	3rd Overtone

And so on...

Fundamental 1st Harmonic	1st Overtone 2nd Harmonic	2nd Overtone 3rd Harmonic	3rd Overtone 4th Harmonic	4th Overtone 5th Harmonic	5th Overtone 6th Harmonic
$A\sharp^1/B\flat^1$	$A\sharp^2/B\flat^2$	F^3	$A\sharp^3/B\flat^3$	D^4	F^4
B^1	B^2	$F\sharp^3/G\flat^3$	B^3	$D\sharp^4/E\flat^4$	$F\sharp^4/G\flat^4$
C^1	C^2	G^3	C^3	E^4	G^4
$C\sharp^1/D\flat^2$	$C\sharp^2/D\flat^3$	$G\sharp^3/A\flat^3$	$C\sharp^3/D\flat^4$	F^4	$G\sharp^4/A\flat^4$
D^2	$D\sharp^3/E\flat^3$	A^3	D^4	$F\sharp^4/G\flat^4$	A^4

Start on Low B-flat
The harmonics of $B\flat^1$ are the easiest to produce. $B\flat^1$ is therefore a good starting point to practice this effect. As you go higher and higher, adjust your tongue, as in saying "ee," and roll your bottom lip slightly outwards (less than one millimeter.)

Artists Who Use Harmonics

Jerry Bergonzi
Daniel Kientzy
Michael Brecker

17. MULTIPHONICS

TRACK 26

Multiphonics are two or more notes sounding at the same time. The notes may be stable or fluctuating. The multiphonic fingerings in the following chart are the fingerings that I find easiest to play on my instruments. *My* best fingerings might not be *your* best fingerings. That's why you can find blank fingering charts in Appendix A, which you can copy and use to track your own best results. I strongly recommend that you experiment and then log your results. It can't be overstressed how important it is to listen to what you are doing, if you want to succeed playing multiphonics. Be patient with yourself!

Tips for Playing and Practicing Multiphonics
- Take only one quarter of the mouthpiece in your mouth.
- Dynamics: Practice playing *p* to *mf*.
- Play with a soft embouchure.
- Sometimes you need to drop your jaw a bit.
- Sometimes you need to tighten the sides of your mouth a bit.

Artists Who Use Multiphonics

Illinois Jacquet
John Coltrane
Michael Brecker

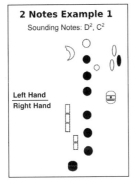

2 Notes Example 1
Sounding Notes: D^2, C^2

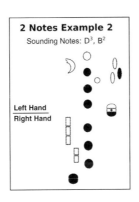

2 Notes Example 2
Sounding Notes: D^3, B^2

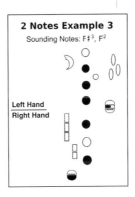

2 Notes Example 3
Sounding Notes: $F\sharp^3$, F^2

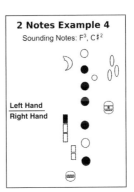

2 Notes Example 4
Sounding Notes: F^3, $C\sharp^2$

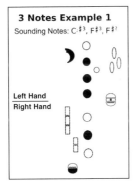

3 Notes Example 1
Sounding Notes: $C\sharp^3$, $F\sharp^3$, $F\sharp^2$

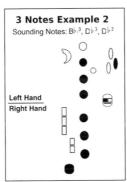

3 Notes Example 2
Sounding Notes: $B\flat^3$, $D\flat^3$, $D\flat^2$

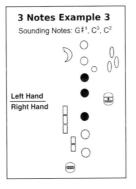

3 Notes Example 3
Sounding Notes: $G\sharp^4$, C^3, C^2

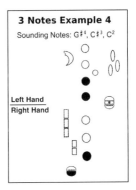

3 Notes Example 4
Sounding Notes: $G\sharp^4$, $C\sharp^3$, C^2

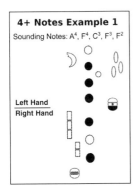

4+ Notes Example 1
Sounding Notes: A^4, F^4, C^3, F^3, F^2

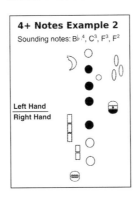

4+ Notes Example 2
Sounding notes: $B\flat^4$, C^3, F^3, F^2

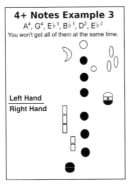

4+ Notes Example 3
A^4, G^4, $E\flat^3$, $B\flat^3$, D^2, $E\flat^2$
You won't get all of them at the same time.

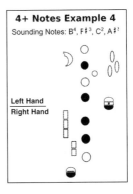

4+ Notes Example 4
Sounding Notes: B^4, $F\sharp^3$, C^2, $A\sharp^2$

18. ALTISSIMO REGISTER

TRACK 27

Using special fingerings, one can expand the regular range of the saxophone quite a bit. Because this is only possible above the highest regular notes this range is called *altissimo register*.

Every saxophone, even ones of the same brand and model, requires slightly different altissimo fingerings. The following fingerings work best for me playing my saxophones. They are a good starting point for you, but I strongly recommend that you experiment and use the fingering chart in the Appendix to log the best fingerings you find for your saxophone.

Altissimo Fingerings for Alto Saxophone

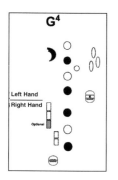
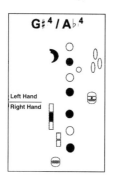
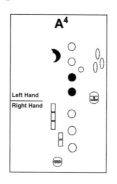
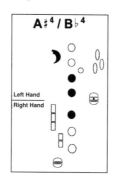
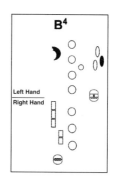
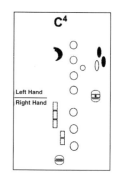

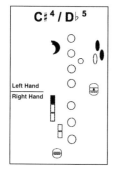
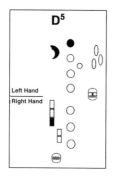
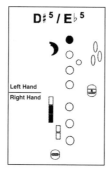
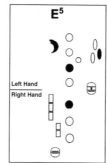
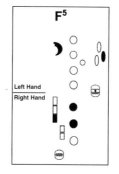

Use the blank fingering charts on page 25 to expand above F5 through experimentation.

Altissimo Fingerings for Tenor Saxophone

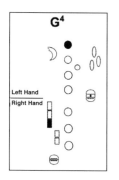
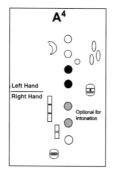
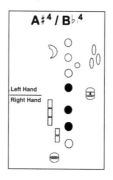
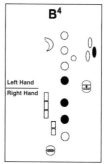
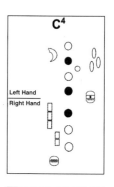

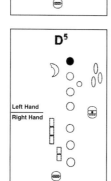
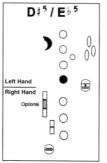
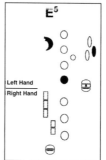
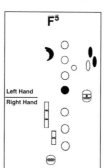

Use the blank fingering charts on page 25 to expand above F5 through experimentation.

Try to relax as much as you can while doing this. The above fingerings are the easy part of altissimo playing. The hard part is to find the right embouchure, air stream support, placement of the mouthpiece, opening of the throat, dynamic, and tongue position *for every note*. Be patient with yourself, as this will take a lot of time and effort. If you get one note a week, then you're on the fast track!

First Harmonics, Then Altissimo

If you have a hard time getting the notes in the altissimo register, work on mastering the harmonics lesson first.

Artists Who Play in the Altissimo Register

Eric Dolphy
John Coltrane
Dave Liebman

19. CIRCULAR BREATHING

TRACK 28

The circular breathing technique allows you to play your saxophone while inhaling through your nose. Picture a bagpipe for a moment. Now replace the pipe with your saxophone and the bag with your cheeks. As you blow your horn, you fill up your cheeks with air. While releasing the air from your cheeks, you breathe in quickly through your nose. During the whole process, you never stop blowing. That's the theory. Now let's practice, using water instead of air in your cheeks.

Take as much water in your mouth as you can. Your cheeks should be fully inflated due to all the water in them. Breathe several times in and out through your nose. Relax. Continue breathing in and out, and start to squirt the water out in a long thin stream. You are now breathing through your nose and releasing water through your mouth. The only difference between what you are doing right now and circular breathing is that you will replace the water with air.

There is another great way to practice circular breathing. Take a glass half full with water and a straw. Blow air through the straw, and inflate your cheeks. Switch from blowing air from your lungs to using the air in your cheeks. At that very moment, you want to inhale as much air as you can through your nose, as quickly as possible. Immediately switch back to blowing air through the straw from your now refilled lungs. Repeat the process as many times as you can.

Once these preliminary exercises work effortlessly, you will be ready to tackle circular breathing on your saxophone. Be aware that this is going to take some time and effort. Start with a single note in the upper register. Remember how your body felt during the exercises, and try to reproduce this feeling. Relax and focus, and you will succeed.

Avoid Fainting!

Take a break if you feel dizzy, and stop immediately if you start hyperventilating!!!

Artists Who Circular Breathe

Rahsaan Roland Kirk
Evan Parker

PART II

Sound Effects Etudes:
Nine Animals

Nine Animals is a composition in nine movements written in the style of program music for saxophone. The basic idea is quite simple: Using the sound effects discussed in this book, try to sound as much as you can like the animals in the compositions. Before every movement, you will find a short scenario that will put you in the mood of the segment.

All songs can be played on E♭ and B♭ saxophones. Just be sure to use the appropriate play-along track.

1. THE ELEPHANT

This elephant is a circus elephant and currently traveling in a train wagon. In the A section, as well as in the F section, the elephant shouts. The train wagon is shaking during the B section and the D section. The elephant is calm and relaxed in the C section and the E section.

Effects Used
• Different Embouchures
• Low "A"
• Vocal Sounds

TRACK 29 TRACK 30 TRACK 31

The Elephant

Ueli Dörig

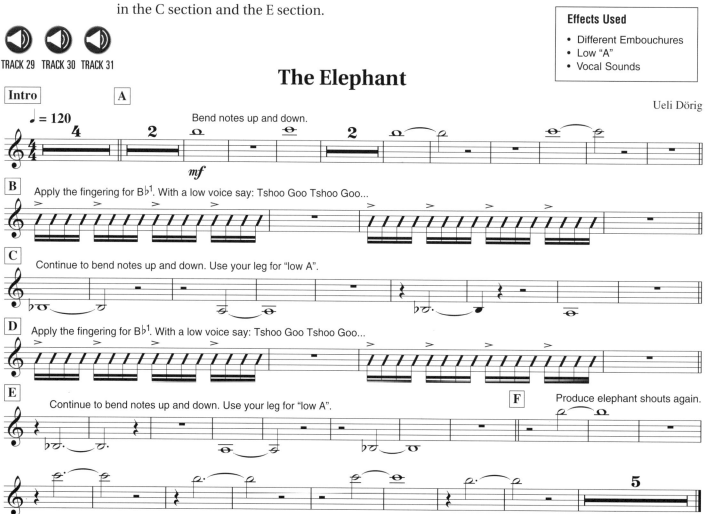

2. THE BACTERIA

What sound does bacteria produce? The sound of multiphonics (MP), of course!
With some imagination you can picture some super-sized "monster bacteria"
from a Hollywood horror movie while playing this movement. Make it as scary
as possible!

Effects Used
- Multiphonics
- Altissimo Register
- Key Clapping

TRACK 32   TRACK 33   TRACK 34

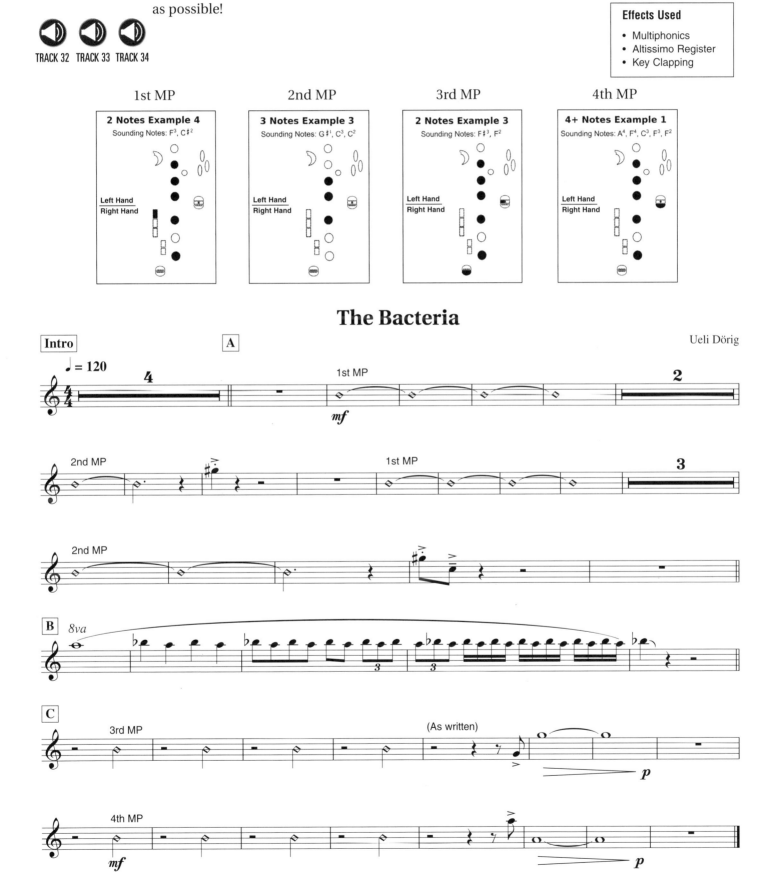

3. THE HORNETS

This movement is for everybody who has ever suffered due to hornets arriving during a summertime garden lunch. Hornets arrive and walk around on the table in the A, C, E, and G sections. In the B, D, and F sections they get more active and aggressive.

TRACK 35   TRACK 36   TRACK 37

Effects Used
- Finger Clicking
- Trills
- Key Clapping

The Hornets

Ueli Dörig

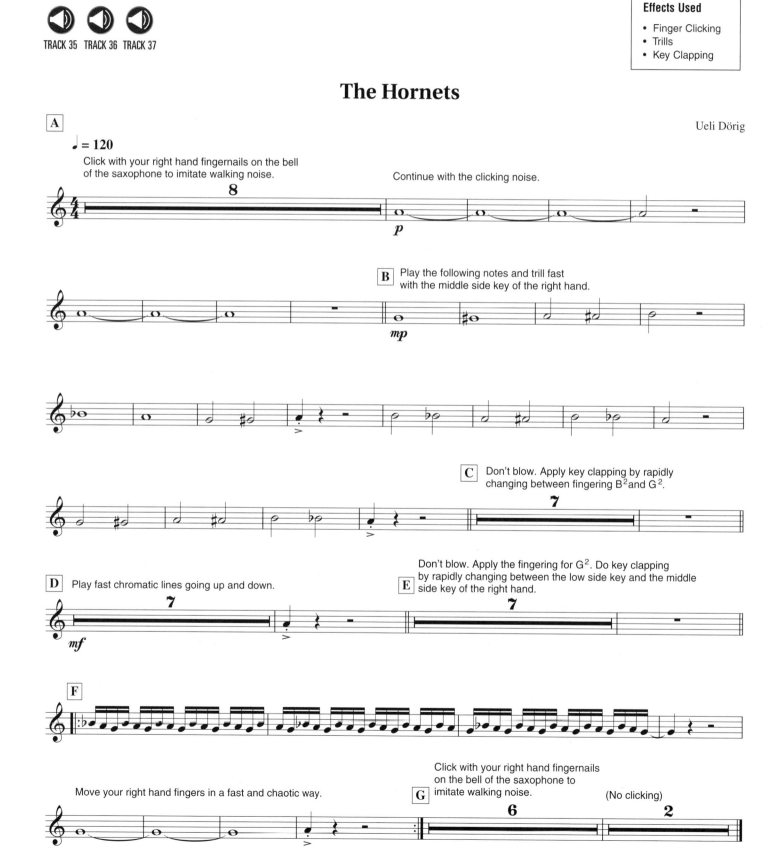

4. THE WHALE

Whenever a whale comes to surface it blows some water out of its breathing hole and takes a deep breath. This is exactly what happens in the A section. In the B section the low notes represent the underwater communication between whales. In the C section the whale stays underwater for a long time without taking a breath. That's why you are not allowed to breathe through your mouth in this section.

TRACK 38 TRACK 39 TRACK 40

Effects Used
- Inhaling and Exhaling Noise
- Circular Breathing

The Whale

Ueli Dörig

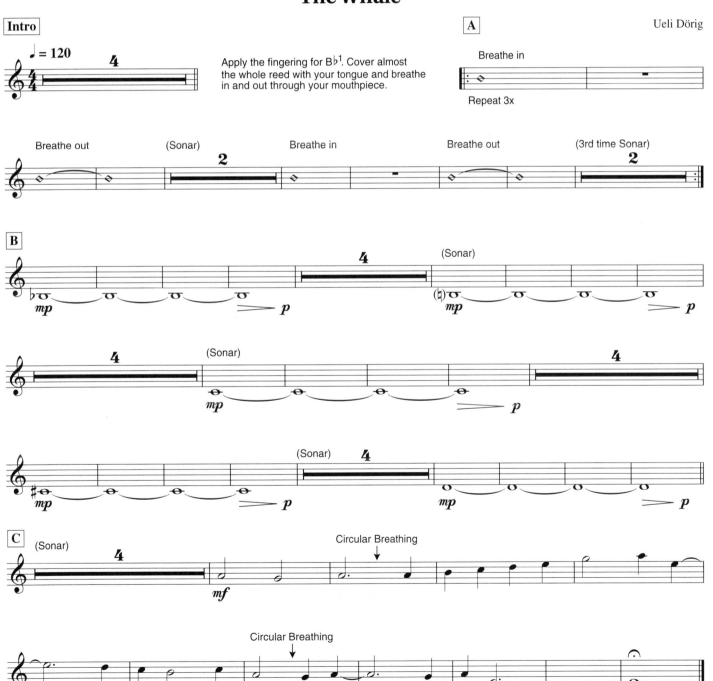

5. THE HORSE

You are going for a ride on a horse, in this movement. In the A section, you get the horse out of the stable and then start to ride it. In the B section, you go cross-country. You ride faster and faster until you, or your horse, are exhausted.

TRACK 41 TRACK 42 TRACK 43

Effects Used
• Double Tonguing
• Flutter Tonguing

The Horse

Ueli Dörig

6. THE MOSQUITO

Imagine that you are lying in your bed during a hot summer night and a really
annoying mosquito arrives. The mosquito flies everywhere in your room during
the A, B, and C section. Sometimes it's closer, and sometimes it's quite far away.
In the D section, you slap the mosquito dead but only on the second time.

TRACK 44   TRACK 45   TRACK 46

Effects Used
- Vibrato
- Key Clapping
- Trills

The Mosquito

Ueli Dörig

7. THE SHARK

This shark approaches quietly, and as it gets closer, it gets louder and more
aggressive. In the B section, the shark disappears but only to come back again!

TRACK 47   TRACK 48   TRACK 49

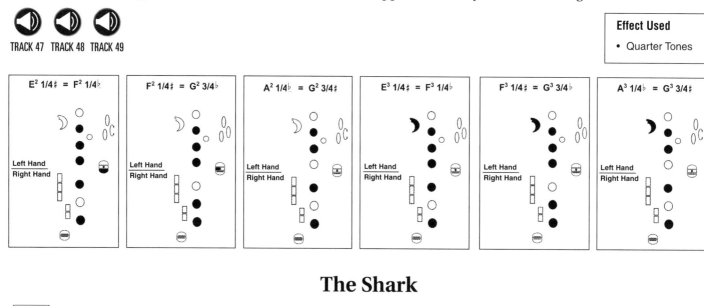

The Shark

Ueli Dörig

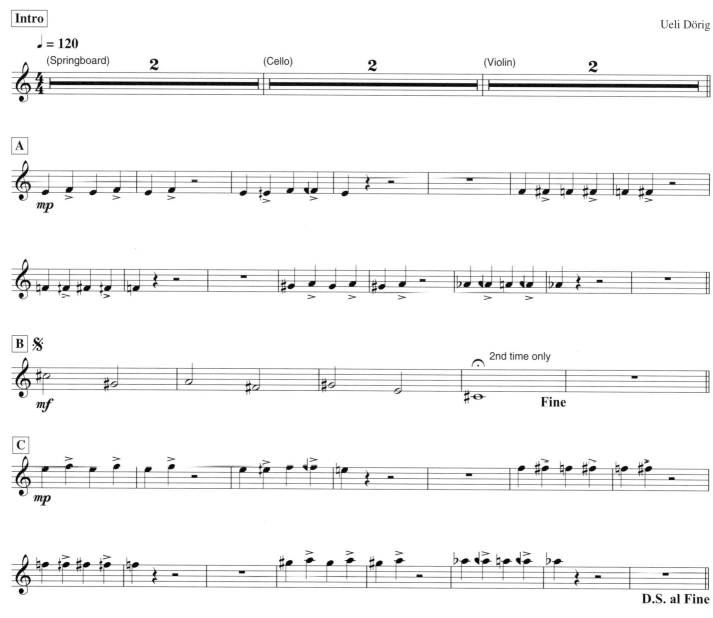

D.S. al Fine

8. THE VAMPIRE BAT

The beating heart that pumps blood through the body is the kind of sound that you want to imitate by slapping the pad against the keyhole in the A section. During the B section and the C section the vampire bat communicates using subsonic sound calls.

TRACK 50   TRACK 51   TRACK 52

Effects Used
- Key Clapping
- Altissimo Register
- Trills

The Vampire Bat

Ueli Dörig

9. THE COBRA

In the first part of the A section, you can hear the cobra flashing its tongue. Later on, the cobra starts to move around. In the B section the cobra is climbing rocks, hiding in bushes, and looking for possible victims. At the end, the cobra finds a mouse, starts to hypnotize it, and finally attacks it.

TRACK 53   TRACK 54   TRACK 55

Effects Used
- Tonguing
- Ghost Notes

The Cobra

APPENDIX A

Blank Fingering Charts

Copy this page of blank charts, and use them to record your own "best" fingerings that you find through experimentation.

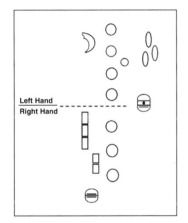
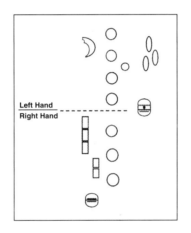
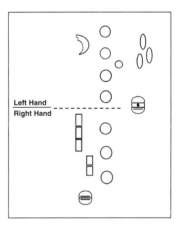

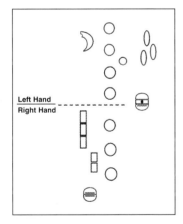
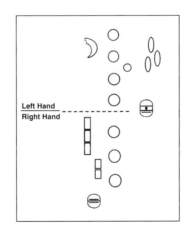
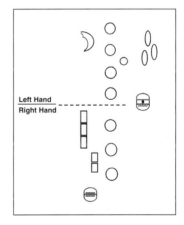

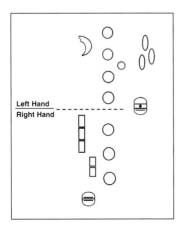
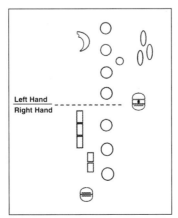
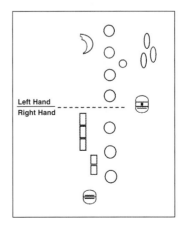

Recommended Reading

Caravan, Ronald L., *Preliminary Exercises & Etudes In Contemporary Techniques For Saxophone*, Medfield, Dorn Publications, 1980. Multiphonics, quarter tones, and timbre variation.

Dörig, Ueli, *www.uelidoerig.com*. Online library with lots of free practice material and free information about everything I know about the musical universe. Check it out!

Gross, John, *Multiphonics for the Saxophone*, Rottenburg, Advance Music, 1998. Multiphonics.

Kientzy, Daniel, *L'art du saxophone*, Paris, Nova-Musica, 1993. Big selection of special effects.

Kientzy, Daniel, *Les sons multiples aux saxophones*, Noisy-le-sec, Salabert Editions, 2003. Multiphonics.

Luckey, Robert A. Ph.D., *Saxophone Altissimo*, Rottenburg, Advance Music, 1992. Overtones and altissimo register.

Rascher, Sigurd M., *Top-Tones for the Saxophone*, New York, Carl Fischer, 1941. Altissimo register.

Anything you can find from Joe Allard, Joseph Viola, Larry Teal, Marcel Mule, and J.M. Londeix.

ABOUT THE AUTHOR

Photo by Martin Cavé

Ueli Dörig is a multi-instrumentalist, music educator, and performing artist. He grew up in Rorschach, Switzerland where he got a bachelor degree in education. After some years of teaching in public school and serving as a Swiss Army musician, he went on to study at the Berklee College of Music, where he graduated magna cum laude in both saxophone performance and jazz composition.

In 2007, Ueli moved to the Ottawa/Gatineau region in Canada where he works as a freelance musician and music educator. Ueli Dörig plays and teaches the saxophone, clarinet, and flute.

Visit **www.uelidoerig.com** for more information about Ueli and to take advantage of a huge library of free information about playing the saxophone and music theory.